IMAGES

of England

HALL GREEN

IMAGES
of England

HALL GREEN

Compiled by
Michael Byrne

Birmingham City Council
Department of Leisure and
Community Services

TEMPUS

First published 1996, reprinted 1998, 2000
Copyright © Michael Byrne, 1996

Tempus Publishing Limited
The Mill, Brimscombe Port,
Stroud, Gloucestershire, GL5 2QG

ISBN 0 7524 0678 7

Typesetting and origination by
Tempus Publishing Limited
Printed in Great Britain by
Midway Clark Printing, Wiltshire

Contents

Acknowledgements   6

Introduction   7

1.   Rural Views   9

2.   The Making of a Suburb   47

3.   Transport   69

4.   Hall Green at Work   79

5.   Portraits   97

6.   Schooldays   105

7.   Social Life   113

Acknowledgements

Inevitably the first source one turns to for the photographic history of a part of Birmingham is the collection of over 200,000 photographs and postcards held in the Central Library. These, and a number from Hall Green Library, form the backbone of the collection shown in this book. However, I have been fortunate to have met many interesting and generous people, who have allowed me to use their precious material and provided information. In particular Karl Thomas, a remarkable postcard collector, stands out as having lent the largest number of pictures for this book. John Bick, another collector, has also been very helpful. Many people are acknowledged in the appropriate captions or below, but I would like to give a special thanks to Peter Bennett, Conrad James, Toni Demidowicz, Mrs Joan Jones, Mrs Joan Woodcock, Mr J. Anthony, Lillian and Barry Mann, Dr Guy Houghton, Norah Clift, Mike and Jean Edwards, Ann Harris, Eileen Goodall, Hall Green Junior School and Mr Waller, Louisa Lacey and Mrs M. Rotton. It has been a delight to get to know Harry Tatton, with his extraordinarily vivid and detailed memories. Hall Green Local History Society have been very supportive, particularly my friends Maurice White (the Society's President) and his wife Ann, who have put in a lot of time to help me. I hope I have accurately represented what everyone has told me: all errors in the book are of course my responsibility. I would like to acknowledge a debt of influence to John Morris Jones, two of whose publications I had the privilege to edit after his death. Other documentary and printed sources are too numerous for me to mention here. I have tried to be sure that I have acknowledged the source of every photograph or postcard not deposited in a public collection or belonging to me. In some cases, where people have loaned material associated with organizations, where I have been lent copies of originals, or where photos are pasted on card, it is possible that I may not have become aware of any copyright holders, and I have no means of knowing whether such rights are held by anyone. Where a name was indicated on an image, I have made every effort to trace it. If I have failed to acknowledge anyone in this book, I apologize here and now.

In the following list of sources, the numbers refer to the pages, 'u' means upper, and 'l' means lower. Gwen Andrew: 45l (via Photo Forum), 46; Mr J. Anthony: 92l; Mr and Mrs A. Beresford and Hall Green Local History Society: 69; John Bick: 74l; Birmingham City Council, City Engineer's Department: 84l; Norah Clift: 99, 100u; Peter Clynes: 116-118u (117 E. Manley); C.H. Coldrick: 40l; Philip Crocker: 20l, 35l, 45u, 71l; Mike and Jean Edwards: 76l, 100l; Graham Gilbert: 112 both; John Gilbert: 86u; Simon Goodman: 94-96; Rick Green: 75l, 76u, 122l; Hall Green Junior School: 106 both, 108u, 109 both; Ann Harris: 101u, 127 (Stanley Hewitt); Mr and Mrs S. Harvey: 128l; Derek Hickson: 111u; Miss Mabel Holden: 111l; Ted Holt: 56l, 61u (S.L. Bowker?), 104l, 120u-122l; Dr Guy Houghton: 17u, 101l-102; Alan Johnson: 110; Joan Jones: 25u; Louisa Lacey: 123-4; Mrs J. Lawrence: 103l; Maureen and Redmond McCusker and Mr and Mrs Cox: 19l; Lillian Mann: 93 both; Reeves collection, Central Library: 80l, 81u, 81l, 82u, 98u; Mrs M. Rotton: 128u; George Smith: 87l-92u; Society of Friends and the late Miss Dorothy J. Dodd: 60l, 125-6; Reta Stiles: 73l; Harry Tatton: 59l, 86l, 107 both, 108l, 119u; Karl Thomas: 25l, 29l, 31, 34u, 43l, 51l, 53l, 60u, 61l, 68l, 70u, 70l, 73u, 74u, 83u, 83l, 84u, 84l, 113; Betty Williams: 36l, 37l, 79, 80u, 97, 98l, 119l; Dick and Barbara Williams: 104u, 114u; Dennis Wragg: 118l

Introduction

Hall Green has evolved from a rural backwater into one of the most desirable places to live in the whole of Birmingham. It became the finest kind of suburb, one which offered affordable status in really pleasant surroundings. A small amount of industrial development took place, with some famous names, but it has never been prominent. The influence of the first Residents' Association in the country, and the attention paid to conservation, have been constant features in Hall Green's development. This book traces in pictures how Hall Green acquired its character, and shows many scenes from the social life of the community, which local people remember so fondly. It contains photographs and postcards from before the turn of the century until 1962.

Hall Green was a small part of the ancient Parish of Yardley, which later became Yardley Rural District. The Parish stretched for seven and a half miles from Yardley Wood to Lea Village. Hall Green has some present-day names which go back to the Middle Ages, like Bromhale and Greet Mill, mentioned in 1275, Haw in 1327 and Six Weyes in 1382. Baldwins Lane, Sarehole Mill, Four Ways, Busmere, Shartmore, Swartmore Laine, and Hawe Green and Hawes House were mentioned in sixteenth century documents. The House became the Hall, and Hawe Green became altered, perhaps inevitably, to Hall Green. Just across from the Hall, Marston Chappell (the Church of the Ascension) was built in Queen Anne's reign. The Hall and the chapel, plus a few houses nearby, made up the late Victorian hamlet. Hall Green has lost this centre, and does not have one today, unless you regard the Stratford Road as an elongated version of one. The old Hall Green of the 1890s was described in a newspaper article as follows. 'It was a quiet country (area) of scattered farms, good-sized houses each surrounded by its own garden… cottages in Church Road and the model village known as the 'hamlet'… As small children we always felt it was a special walk if we had seen Mr and Mrs Heath drive out between the tall iron gates (of Hall Green Hall) or received their kindly smile as they drove soberly past… Another favourite walk along lanes, sweet in summer with dog-rose and honeysuckle, was to the farm beside the race-course, where Mrs Hyatt sometimes produced glasses of foamy milk from the cool dairy or some of her home-brewed ginger beer. Of all lonely spots in Hall Green this would seem to have been the loneliest, for Mrs Hyatt's husband had only once in his life been in a train, and her brother who lived with them had never seen train or tram…'

The early years of the twentieth century brought change. Rail passenger services came to Hall Green and Yardley Wood in 1908, and terraced housing began to appear at the Sparkhill end of the area. In 1911 Hall Green, along with the rest of Yardley Rural District, voted to be absorbed into the city of Birmingham, which promised better infrastructure and services. The Severne family sold their Hall Green Estate in 1912, and in 1913 the last manorial lands, the Taylor Estate, were put on the market. Trams came over the river Cole to the Bull's Head from 1914. In 1928 they went on to the city boundary, and the 29 bus service to Highfield Road began. Everything was in place for the great transformation, and housing appeared all over the area. However, something rather special happened. What characterized the inter-war urbanization of Hall Green was not only the great proportion of private housing but the quantity of green space remaining enclosed behind the new dwellings. Since 1945, however, further more intensive development has been a constant threat to this greenest of green suburbs. Large houses have been pulled down and replaced by groups of small townhouses or flats, and nurseries, sports grounds, unused areas behind gardens, and even long gardens themselves, have been targeted by developers. The fight to preserve Hall Green's character goes on unabated today.

One of the most attractive areas in the whole of the city is in Hall Green: the Cole valley from the Solihull border to the Stratford Road. The city has kept faith with early plans to keep this green corridor free of further development. Today's local conservationists formed the River Cole and Chinn Brook Conservation Group in 1985. This summer they achieved the long-held goal, supported by the city's Millstream Project, of an uninterrupted river walkway from Solihull Lodge through to the Ackers and beyond. The Group argues strongly for nature conservation in the valley, and also seeks the preservation of old hedgerows, fragments of ancient woodland, and other remnants of historic landscape. These are present as 'time-slips' amidst the later developments, and the group aims to make people aware of them and value them.

With all this talk of conservation and green space, it may not be recognized that Hall Green has an interesting industrial past. Before the suburbs came, of course, there were smithies, and mills, some of which ground blades or rolled metal. Some of the more recent industrial activity was also there before the houses. Early Ordnance Survey maps show a small building set in fields, called the Robin Hood Works. This became Newey Goodman, manufacturers of 'smallwares' such as pins and grips. A small chocolate factory appeared on its own at Webb Lane in 1911, where fork-lift trucks and other electric vehicles were later produced. Aldis Brothers built a factory on a green field site in 1914 at Sarehole Road, and made world famous signalling lamps. York Road was home to one of Britain's foremost motorcycling names, Velocette. Maybe it is time to honour this local industrial heritage, now that it is slipping from sight and memory. There are still a few rows of workshops left, and Lucas Aerospace remains at York Road, but Hedges' L260 snuff factory, a local curiosity, has gone.

There are other famous names associated with Hall Green. Comedian Tony Hancock was born on Southam Road, the author J.R.R. Tolkien lived near Sarehole Mill as a small boy, and Nigel Mansell, one of Britain's greatest racing drivers, spent nearly all his childhood and his early adult years in Hall Green.

Local history is important in giving a sense of time and place, in helping those who come to live in an area to develop an identification with it, and an identity in it. For the purposes of this book, the boundary of Hall Green is defined as follows. Starting at the river bridge at the Stratford Road, a line runs southwards roughly via Shaftmoor Lane and York Road on to Lakey Lane and the city boundary. It goes along the city boundary westwards as far as the river, then turns back north along the Cole walkway to the Stratford Road. This may not tie in exactly with postcodes or political boundaries, but I make no apology for including the historic riverside areas of Trittiford and Sarehole in Hall Green. I hope this collection of images from the past gives pleasure and information to those who take an interest in Hall Green's past, and its future.

Almost half the photographs and postcards included here came from the extensive collection in Birmingham Central Library. Even that has gaps, though. If anyone has material they would like to see made more widely available, the Local Studies and History section would be very grateful to hear from them on 0121-235 4549.

One
Rural Views

Cart shed, Shaftmoor Lane, *c.* 1910. Described as a 'waggon hovel' in the mid-nineteenth century Tithe Award, this humble structure is here the centrepiece of a lovely rural scene. The cart shed belonged to Shaftmoor Farm.

Shaftmoor, *c.* 1895. The estate was owned for over two hundred years by the Steedman family. This Tudor timber-framed building was demolished in December 1929, with some panelling going to Packwood House. Phillip Steedman continued in the outbuildings with his garage, later Elt Bros.

The cart shed and farm outbuildings, November 1923. Houses are already standing behind the photographer (see opposite and p. 48), and there is a new bus route along here going between Moseley and Erdington, split in 1926 into parts of the No. 1 and Outer Circle routes.

Shaftmoor Lane, 1924. Across the road from Shaftmoor, new council houses are about to be built. 'Bricklayers wanted, long job', the board says.

Phillip Steedman's garage, and the new estate, 11 September 1924. The houses in the background have been there two decades.

Kings Farm, or Greet Mill Hill Farm, Shaftmoor Lane, c. 1910. This stood at the top of the slope down to the Stratford Road. Valoric A. Luck began his timber business here in 1926 (see p. 92), and Billingsley's dairy operated from here from around 1922 to 1936. The farmhouse was replaced by Christadelphian offices in the early 1960s.

Job Marston's chapel on a card posted on 24 December 1906. This postcard shows a perfect rural scene, taken from Fox Hollies Road, with the drive to Hall Green Hall on the left.

The church from the field at the corner of Fox Hollies Road, 1912. It was built with money provided in the will of Job Marston, who died in 1701 and who lived at Hall Green Hall across the way. His bequest also paid for the incumbent's salary. The church was consecrated in 1704 as Marston Chappell. Job Marston's chapel was built with small hand-made bricks, and features round-headed windows, stone quoins, a balustrade and a copper-domed bell cupola. The architect was Sir William Wilson. Between 1860 and 1866 it was extended, with north and south transepts and a new chancel. The extension does not have a balustrade, but the newer bricks and overall design are in keeping. Not surprisingly, it is a listed building. It was restored from 1951-2. The chapel became Hall Green Parish church in 1907, then was renamed the Church of the Ascension on its 250th Anniversary on 25 May 1954, as a second parish, St Peter's, was to be created in Hall Green. At the same time, the foundation stone for Chatterton Hall was laid. This commemorated the outstanding ministry of Revd Percy Chatterton, curate from 1932-8, and vicar from then until 1952, when he had to resign the living due to ill-health caused by prolonged overwork. He died on Easter Day in 1954, aged only forty-four.

Hall Green Hall on a card posted in 1910. Parts of the Hall dated back to the fifteenth and sixteenth centuries. The arrival of the wealthy Job Marston in 1683 led to more additions. He probably had the farm buildings rebuilt, and may have had a separate farmhouse added, so that the timber-framed hall could serve exclusively as his home. *Architect and Building News*, in their 'Obituaries of Buildings' feature on Hall Green Hall, referred to the brick wing as Georgian, writing of highly interesting additions made towards the end of the eighteenth century, i.e. while the Wigleys owned the hall. The wing contained a staircase-hall with a continuous cantilevered landing approached by way of a staircase with divided flights, with great subtlety of design. Bedrooms and other rooms were off the landing. Adam ceilings and fireplaces were put in, and the Georgian Gothic style windows were added to the timber-framed parts of the Hall as well. Job Marston was a bachelor, and his property passed in a series of indirect inheritances to the Wigley family and then by marriage to the Severne family, who sold their Hall Green Estate in 1912. The Hall stood left of the end of a drive opposite the church. It was sold around 1935 by the Lloyd family. They were dismayed by the sight of the new Dare's semis on former Hall Farm land, which were beginning to surround their home, and by the conversion of the Hall and farm drives to 'School Road'. The new owners sold the Hall on, and it was demolished and replaced by the fine Charles Lane Trust almshouses. The Trust was set up on the death of Charles Lane of the Beeches (see p. 58), who started with horse buses and became a transport entrepreneur and wealthy property owner. Ironically School Road and Miall Road are now a conservation area, that of an inter-war suburb. It was a good place for the city to choose, because the conservation area not only includes the Dare's Distinctive Houses, with one pair of 'suntrap' houses and typical inter-war shops, but also a 1930s pub design, the Three Magpies, and the almshouses. The latter look ancient but date from 1936. If the Hall had survived, it and the church would be the clear historic focus of Hall Green. The almshouses cannot pretend to be part of that.

The Hall in 1934.

The entrance to the Hall, 1934.

Hall Green Hall Farm, 1912.

The Hall Farm, 1935. School Road has now been cut in front of the farmhouse, and houses stand opposite.

Three of the Houghton boys on Fox Hollies Road with Nellie Chandler, *c.* 1916. Nellie was the family's maid. A.C. (Micky) and Cuthbert Roy are having a ride in panniers, while Cuthbert Colin is walking alongside. Dr Cuthbert Houghton kept this donkey on fields where Brooklands Road is now. See pp. 101-2 for more on the Houghton family.

Church Lane, *c.* 1905. Until around 1910 this was the name for the stretch of Fox Hollies Road from the church to the Stratford Road. From then until around 1914 it was known as Church Road.

Church Road, *c.* 1912. Later versions of this postcard are renamed Fox Hollies Road. The houses were part of the Hall Green Estate, and stood between School Road and Lakey Lane opposite the church. They were demolished around 1936 for road widening when only three decades old.

The Hamlet, *c.* 1900. A group of substantial houses were built by the Severnes in the 1880s and 1890s from the Stratford Road to Fox Hollies Road, along Hamlet Road. Plaques remind us who built them. The Friends Meeting House was also part of this development, built as a reading room for the Hamlet.

The shop at the corner of Boden Road, *c.* 1936. This part of Fox Hollies Road was not widened until a few years before the Second World War, later than the stretch from the church to Acocks Green. This shop would now be in the central reservation.

Hall Green Post Office, *c.* 1900. From 1898 the directories show Caleb Cox now running the post office, with butchers and grocers businesses added. The family's descendants in Quebec gave a copy of this photo to Maureen and Redmond McCusker, who helped them with their family history when they visited Hall Green.

Hall Green Post Office, *c.* 1912. From 1911-14, the directories show Caleb Cox running the post office and a cycle repair business. This building stood where the end of Peverell Drive is now. The boundary wall of the Beeches is on the left.

The Horse Shoes pub, *c.* 1905. An inn was listed here in the 1881 census. Local residents will note with gratitude that its brief career in the 1980s as a plastic fun pub with the name of Toad Hall is slipping further into the past. The former Charity School can be seen beyond the pub.

Layston Lodge, 1912. This stood south of the inn. It was built by 1895 and had the customary stables, coach house, and servants' 'offices' 'shut off'. It and Doriscourt below were sold by the Severnes in 1912. Flats now stand in place of the two properties.

Doriscourt, 1912. This imposing house was also built by 1895, and stood just south of Layston Lodge. It had four bedrooms on the first floor, three servants' bedrooms on the second floor, domestic offices as above, stable, coach-house and harness room, and a large garden with a tennis lawn.

Cole Bank Road, January 1923. The river bridge was replaced in that year. On the left, a spillway from one of the headraces to Sarehole Mill came down to the river. Parts of it are still visible, for example at the start of the John Morris Jones Way.

Cole Bank Road looking to the Stratford Road, 1923. The sign says: 'This bridge is insufficient to carry weights beyond the ordinary traffic of the district'.

Sarehole Mill and pool, c. 1905. This is the only surviving operational water mill in Birmingham, out of more than five dozen. This view is of the rebuild of around 1770, plus the barn, and the engine house and chimney added in the mid-nineteenth century for steam power. The mill pool originally received water from the Coldbath Brook only, via a storage pool on the other side of Wake Green Road. This was drained round the turn of the century and is now known as Moseley Bog, although it should really be called Wake Green Bog, as Moseley is some distance away and was in a different Parish altogether. The former storage pool is now a Local Nature Reserve. Matthew Boulton's father tenanted the mill from 1756, dying in 1759, and his son, who became one of the greatest entrepreneurs and industrialists of his age, moved to Soho Mill in 1761. Just think, instead of the Soho Manufactory we might have had the Sarehole Manufactory, and pilgrims would have come here to see one of the most important sites in the early Industrial Revolution. Hall Green would have been a very different place in those circumstances! Richard Eaves, the owner of the mill, began to take out loans three years after Matthew Boulton left, and an additional supply of water was made by around 1768 along a half-mile leat beginning at the 'Whyrl-Hole' bridge in the Dingles. Blade grinding, by no means an unusual function for a rural water mill, was undertaken for a few decades towards the end of the eighteenth century. George Andrew Snr used the mill for his bone-grinding and manure manufacturing business until 1919. His son, George Junior, became a florist. The greenhouse was already there by 1915. After his death in 1959 the mill passed to the city. A solicitor, A.H. Foster, who had bought the mill and meadows from the Taylor estate, prevented development on the land, and bequeathed it to the city. The gift took effect on the death of the miller's son. Sarehole Mill was nearly lost to vandals. Campaigners fought successfully for its restoration, and it was opened as a museum in 1969. It is now a popular educational and tourist attraction. (See p. 26 for a connection with J.R.R. Tolkien.)

Sarehole Mill, 1933.

Green Lane on a card posted on 6 April 1922. Part of the Chalet is timber-framed under the Victorian additions. The outbuilding's timber framing can be seen. Both structures are listed.

24

Green Lane footbridge, *c.* 1930. Today's unattractive metal and concrete bridge is on the north side of the road. The level of the ford was raised here in 1972, but had to be lowered again in 1974, as one of the wheels at the mill would no longer turn, with the tailrace fall having become inadequate.

Green Lane ford looking east towards the Stratford Road, *c.* 1910. Sarehole Road was not extended past here until the 1930s, and was meant to be part of a riverside highway from Trittiford to Greet. The through route was never completed.

Wake Green Road at Sarehole, *c.* 1910. J.R.R. Tolkien, world-famous author of *The Hobbit* and the *Lord of the Rings* trilogy, lived at 5 Gracewell, on the left, from 1896-1900, between the ages of four and eight. In an interview in 1966 reproduced in the *Guardian* in 1991, he described how important the little country hamlet of Sarehole had been in the development of his fictional vision: 'It was a kind of lost paradise … There was an old mill that really did grind corn with two millers, a great big pond with swans on it, a sandpit, a wonderful dell with flowers, a few old-fashioned village houses and, further away, a stream with another mill … I could draw you a map of every inch of it. I loved it with an (intense) love … I was brought up in considerable poverty but I was happy running about in that country. I took the idea of the hobbits from the village people and children … ' George Andrew, who often chased the young Tolkien off his property while covered in dust from his bone-grinding, became the 'White Ogre'. Moseley Bog is recalled in 'Old Forest'. Tolkien was unaware of the blade-grinding past of Sarehole Mill, and he did not like suburbia. He contributed money to the restoration fund. Ironically it was suburbanites, led by people like John Morris Jones, who saved the mill with their campaign.

Sarehole Farm, 1932. In the early eighteenth century the Eaves family owned the farm as well as Sarehole Mill. It was known then as Sarehole Hall. The Boulton family lived there while at Sarehole Mill. The farm was rebuilt in the early nineteenth century, and was part of the Taylor Estate when it was sold in 1913.

A view towards Wake Green Road and Sarehole Garage, formerly Sarehole Farm, 9 March 1933. The farmhouse itself was finally demolished around 1957. Some of the outbuildings survived in the transport yard behind the Woodlands Garage, its later name, until a few years ago.

Wake Green Road looking back from Four Arches Bridge, 21 March 1933. Coming south to here, Wake Green Road used to run down to a ford at the river after bending left where the prefabs are now, then continued on up the west bank to Four Arches Bridge. Much of that stretch has been rediscovered under decades of growth, restored and named as part of the John Morris Jones Way, after the late and much missed local historian. The farm building belongs to Brook Farm. The headrace to Sarehole Mill runs under the bridge seen here. Its line used to be visible in front of the semis on Wake Green Road until sewer works obliterated it. Access to the riverside here is now along Coleside Avenue, with a pleasant sheltered housing development alongside. This replaced other prefabs. Wake Green Road's prefabs are of an uncommon type, the Phoenix, are rare survivals, and are now listed buildings.

The river Cole and Brook Farm on a card sent on 27 February 1906.

A gorgeous scene showing the ford at Four Arches Bridge at the turn of the century. Note that the area was thought to be part of Yardley Wood, a name now associated with inter-war council estates rather than with the large part of Yardley Manor formerly covered by woodland.

Four Arches Bridge, *c.* 1920. The junction of old Brook Lane, Webb Lane, and Wake Green Road at the ford shows why this spot was a favourite place for outings.

Ladies at leisure, horse traffic and bicycles, with Brook Farm in the background, *c.* 1905.

Four Arches Bridge and Webb Lane, on a card posted in 1905. This view was sold as a coloured postcard. The simple rails on the earlier picture have been replaced by these attractive cross-timbered ones. Webb Lane, named after the family that owned Brook Farm in the early nineteenth century, came straight down to the ford until the 1906 railway embankment cut it and Robin Hood Lane off. The two lanes were then brought together to go under a single bridge. People still used the old Webb Lane route by climbing over the railway embankment until houses on Cole Valley Road were built. The former line of Robin Hood Lane was down today's Robin Hood Crescent and part of Marion Way to the ford mentioned on pp. 28 and 73. The hedgerow along there is the original one, according to Peter Bennett of the River Cole and Chinn Brook Conservation Group.

Brook Farm and the Bridge, *c.* 1930. By the time this picture was taken, the bridge rails had gone, and the farm itself had only a few years left. Part of the farm became a sweet shop before its demolition. After further damage and decay, the bridge was restored in the mid-1950s as a result of a campaign.

The back of Brook Farm from old Brook Lane, 1932. This lane is now a footpath and today's Colebourne Road. New Brook Lane was not cut until the 1930s, as part of an ambitious plan for a tram route from Quinton to Olton. Wake Green Road was extended on a new line to meet it. See also p. 42.

Looking up old Brook Lane, 1935. Some of these trees remain.

A path through the Dingles, 1935. This tree at the corner of old Brook Lane still stands. The miller at Sarehole would have been obliged to provide the little bridge over his new headrace around 1768 in order to restore an early footpath, perhaps between Paradise Farm and Billesley Farm. Both bridge and channel are still visible.

The Dingles on a card posted in April 1912.

The Dingles, c. 1905. This area was also seen as being associated with Moseley as well as Hall Green and Yardley Wood. The Dingles walk is beautiful, and I have seen a kingfisher flash past me on more than one occasion.

Highfield Road river bridge looking through to Trittiford Mill, 12 August 1924. The large pool nearby was embanked and dug out around 1783 for the mill, and was bought by the city in 1923.

Trittiford Mill, c. 1910. There are many versions of the name, some amusing. There were farm buildings and a house in addition to the mill itself. See also p. 82.

Trittiford Mill, 1932. Chas. B. Davis, portable buildings, is in business. Around 1937, Trittiford Road was completed through the site, to Highfield Road. The mill buildings, occupied at the time by J.W. Halmshaw, general dealer, had been destroyed by fire on 17 February 1926.

Trittiford Farm, *c.* 1910, soon after the Reeves family took up residence. They were here from 1909-37. There are several photos of the family and the work at the farm in this book.

Trittiford Farm, 27 January 1937. Yardley Wood Library, much demanded by Hall Green residents, was opened at the end of 1936, and is visible behind the farm. Wider versions of School Road and Highfield Road were supposed to link up eventually over the farm site, but this was not done.

The demolition of the barn at Trittiford Farm, 10 January 1935. The old man on the left is Thomas Reeves Snr.

The Bull's Head, *c.* 1910. The corner of the Beeches can be seen on the left, soon to be the home of Charles Lane.

The Bull's Head hotel seen from Highfield Road, 1912. This picture was taken for the Hall Green Estate sale catalogue. This building dates from around 1840, and may be a likely candidate for the site of the oldest inn in the area, being at Four Ways, the junction of the ridgeway to Yardley and the road to Stratford. At the time of sale, the inn had farm buildings including several cart sheds, three piggeries, two cow-houses, two stables, and a harness room.

Hall Green House. This stood on the north side of Highfield Road at the Stratford Road, and was occupied by the Rock family. Mrs Rock outlived her husband by many years. Hall Green House became a private school for a while in the early 1920s, and was later demolished to make way for the shops (see p. 59).

Hillclose Farm, c. 1910. The Dolphin family moved here from Swanshurst around 1854. This attractive farmhouse stood on Highfield Road opposite Webb Lane. It was demolished around 1920.

Robin Hood Farm, *c.* 1910. This stood on the Stratford Road just south of Baldwins Lane. The board advertises Waites' ginger beer. The road was widened here in 1923, and this whole area was swallowed up by the biggest roundabout in Birmingham in 1933.

Robin Hood Lane on a card posted on 22 August 1910. Cut flowers are on sale at the cottage.

An old cottage in Robin Hood Lane, August 1931.

Highfield Road with a view of the smithy/wheelwright's business at the corner of Webb Lane, *c.* 1920. The owner's name was Sparks!

The smithy, *c.* 1920. It operated until around 1939, and the buildings survived until around 1956, when they were replaced by two bungalows.

Looking towards Kings Heath from the railway embankment, 3 December 1932. Cole Valley Road is on the left, there is no extended Sarehole Road or new Brook Lane yet, and Wake Green Road is on its old line just beyond the low river bridge. The sign announces the new Sarehole Garage business.

Land for sale at the junction of Webb Lane and Robin Hood Lane, 26 January 1925.

Baldwins Lane on a card posted in July 1908. The black and white house is now the veterinary surgery, and has been painted all one colour.

Scribers Lane ford, *c.* 1900. Just south of Trittiford Pool is the ford at Scribers Lane. This is another view well represented in photographs and postcards, and this one is particularly attractive. Because of wear to the ford approaches, the river turned west before resuming its journey northwards, making the ford wide and shallow. This is deceptive. After heavy rain the river can rise very quickly, and cars attempting to cross are sometimes swept downstream. There is a spillway from the pool's headrace at the ford. Looking at the bridge today, its arches date from the early nineteenth century, but the brickwork above has been replaced, and the large pipe alongside is an eyesore. On Scribers Lane opposite Barton Lodge Road, the farmhouse of Yew Tree Farm survives, much altered. It may date from the late eighteenth century.

Scribers Lane ford and cottages, *c.* 1910. The cottages were subject to being flooded when the river was high. Harry Tatton recalls coming past here and seeing the inhabitants looking out from upstairs as the water surged past above the level of the downstairs windows. Not surprisingly, the cottages have gone.

Slade Lane ford, looking west, 1933. When in flood, the river rose over the top of this wooden footbridge. The new bridge is on the south side of the lane.

Slade Lane ford, 1936. This photo was taken by Mrs Gwen Andrew as a young girl. She had just received a present of a new bicycle, a Coventry Three Spires with three Sturmey Archer gears, costing £3 19s 11d. She recalls often going down to the railway bridge just behind where this view was taken to see the colony of bats take off in the evening. She told me that gypsies' horses from their camp at Scribers Lane used to come up what became Barton Lodge Road, and once ate the newly planted hedges in the gardens at the bottom of Baldwins Lane. Gwen Andrew also recalls a pig farm over the river on the north side, where the breakers' yard is now. As can be seen from her photograph, the gravel ford was wider and deeper than today's concrete version. The headrace to Trittiford Mill begins on the far side of the ford, but, curiously, upstream of the lane: a bridge had to be provided at the miller's expense.

Two

The Making of a Suburb

THE NEW BRIDGE STRATFORD ROAD

The new bridge at the river Cole on a card posted on 18 October 1914. Before trams could penetrate into Hall Green, the two narrow bridges, one over the river channel, the other over the millrace from Greet Mill, had to be replaced. The remains of the mill were found as work progressed to restore a single river channel. Trams crossed from 31 May 1914, but the bridge was formally opened on 20 July.

Shaftmoor Lane, *c.* 1910. Russell Road is on the right, and Springcroft Road on the left of this view of the first part of the lane to be built up.

New prefabs at Colgreave Avenue, 24 April 1946. Behind is the 1933 U.R./Moravian church, built on the site of the former steam tram depot (see p. 69). A piece of tramline is still visible to the side of the church, and, appropriately perhaps, the organist uses an old tram mirror.

Sarehole Road from Dunsmore Road to the Stratford Road, *c.* 1914. This was as far as the road got before the First World War. Aldis Brothers set up their factory in 1914 behind where this view was taken from. They were outstandingly skilled optical manufacturers, and their signalling lamps from 1916 dominated seafaring worldwide for decades, and were also used on airfields and in naval battles. The company left in 1967, and the brand name has only just expired within the Rank Organization. The factory was demolished in 1987 and replaced by Aldis Close.

Terraces on the west side of the Stratford Road, *c.* 1910. The postal address at the time was Greet Mill Hill.

Green Bank from the north, *c.* 1905. This stood opposite the terraces over the page, where the petrol station is now. Some trees from the grounds survive in the grassed area between Reddings Lane and the Stratford Road.

Reddings Lane, *c.* 1905. The wall to Green Bank is on the left. Often there are only a couple of children or a cart on a postcard: here the photographer has assembled quite a crowd.

Green Road on a card posted on 21 September 1929.

Cateswell House, 1932. This stood opposite Cateswell Road at the Stratford Road. It was built in the mid-nineteenth century. Many local people remember it because it was the headquarters of the 48th (1st) Signallers, Territorial Army from 1931. Before that it had been a girls' school from 1919. After the Second World War, dances were held in the drill hall, with Les Williams and his orchestra. Following later use by the Technical College, Cateswell House was demolished in the 1980s.

The Hazelmoor Cafe, corner of the Stratford Road and Cole Bank Road, 1935. This stood where the parking bay is at the junction. See also p. 85.

The old railway bridge on Cole Bank Road, 26 March 1931. The bridge was replaced in 1937. To the right was Kyotts Lake House, home of the garage owner William Henry Edwards (see p. 85). Cole Bank Tennis Club was accommodated in his grounds. The house was renamed Cambrai House when used by the Signallers after his death. Hall Green College was built on the site in 1960. The original owners, the Simcox family, brought the name Kyotts Lake with them from Camp Hill.

Southam Road with a horse-drawn bakery vehicle, *c.* 1910. Houses were soon built to complete the road on the right down to Green Road. Number 41, just to the right of the photographer, is a place of pilgrimage for fans of Tony Hancock, who was born there on 12 May 1924. He moved to the south at the age of three.

Southam Road, bomb damage, 3 January 1941.

Cole Bank Road, 10 October 1935.

Wake Green Road at Gracewell Road, 1935. The building on the left is Mrs Evelyn Edwards' shop. She stayed until around 1938. The shop has been demolished.

Fox Hollies Road, 13 August 1923. This stretch of the road will be widened first, by mid-1931. The house rows with projecting wings are of a design popular with the city in the early 1920s.

Fox Hollies Road at York Road, 2 May 1929. The 'Ninestiles walk' crossed here on its way out to the city boundary at Gospel Lane and beyond.

Lakey Lane, *c.* 1925. School Road has not yet been cut to join the lane just beyond these new houses, and Bushmore Road and the Pitmaston council estate do not yet exist.

Prefabs at Lakefield Close, *c.* 1950. Alongside here ran the drive to Broom Hall, a moated farmhouse rebuilt in the eighteenth century. After Mrs Izod left and local children used the house as a den. In the days of rationing, the provisions abandoned there were an attraction. The house was demolished around 1947, and the area covered by the extension to Edenbridge Road in 1951.

Shirley Road at Lakey Lane, looking south, 30 July 1931. Behind the houses, where Bushmore Road is being built, there used to be a racecourse and a small golf course. The racecourse lasted until around 1911 and the Robin Hood golf course until around 1918. The golf course reappeared in the directories at Gospel Lane from 1930. Dyke Wilkinson wrote thus of the racecourse: 'few beyond Birmingham sportsmen patronised it, but they attended in such enormous numbers that, with a certain class of Birmingham folk, it got to be called their 'Derby Day' ... Many of the roughest of Birmingham roughs attended these races, and I have witnessed deplorable doings there ... ' No wonder that Hall Green School on the Stratford Road used to close, or close early, on race days! The builder's board invites you to come and reside at Hall Green, Birmingham's healthiest suburb, where you can now get distinctively designed semi-detached residences with three reception and four bedrooms, electrically equipped with light and power, with brick garages and four hundred square yard gardens, all for £750-£825!

The Stratford Road at Fox Hollies Road, 2 July 1935. The house at the corner is the Beeches, home of Charles Lane from 1913 until his death in 1933. Fox Hollies Road will be widened in a year's time.

The Stratford Road by Highfield Road, c. 1925. Harry Tatton (centre) assures me that he and his friends did not want to be photographed. On the left is Bill Elt, related to the builder and Councillor B.D. Elt of Yardley Rural District Council and Sparkhill Ward, and on the right is Fred Cox.

Highfield Road from the Stratford Road, 25 June 1924. Hall Green House was on the right (see p. 39).

The same view, 19 September 1933. It can be seen that some of the trees were retained, no doubt as a result of the Residents' Association's efforts from 1925 as well as the city's own policies declared in the post-1918 South Birmingham Town Planning Scheme.

The Parade near Baldwins Lane, *c.* 1927. Note which way the van is facing: see p. 77. Harvey's confectioners has a Cosy Tea Room. The tramlines will come in 1928.

The Birches, *c.* 1912. This was the home of the Smith family at the time. Some pictures of them are in the section on social life. The first listing as a garage is in 1927, with a bazaar as well from 1933-6.

The Auxiliary Fire Service at the Birches, 1940. Division Five, Station Two featured in the June 1940 edition of *Squirt*, the official journal of the Birmingham AFS. The house can be seen behind the garage: it lasted until the late 1950s.

Ingestre Road from the Stratford Road, *c.* 1935.

Shirley Road at the Robin Hood pub, *c.* 1931. There used to be a small inn up the road here, which gave the whole area its name, and later a gasworks built, appropriately, by a Thomas Fitter, for his mansion. Robin Hood House was converted into a pub when the tramlines were extended to the city boundary.

Solihull Lane, 1931.

The Stratford Road near Robin Hood Lane, 11 January 1923. Soon the first stage of the transformation of this road into the congested urban highway of today will begin.

Robin Hood Lane at the Stratford Road, 27 January 1925. The police station, which used to be a house called the Oaks, is on the left. Road widening has removed the grounds and drive formerly in front of the house. The police left in November 1974, and the building became a restaurant. Harry Tatton recalls that the remains of a biplane were kept within the grounds on the right of this picture.

The Stratford Road at Robin Hood Lane, 26 January 1925. Until 1933 there was a series of small islands at the junction, plus tramlines from 1928, making it rather complicated to negotiate.

Robin Hood Lane looking back to the Stratford Road, 13 May 1931.

Robin Hood Lane, 1932. Unemployed men were used to widen the road. The clump of trees is still there, by today's Sherwood Close.

Robin Hood Lane looking east, at Primrose Lane, 27 January 1925.

Robin Hood Lane at Highfield Road, 26 January 1925. Highfield House is just to the right.

Baldwins Lane, 2 July 1934. This is the row of houses opposite the shops, looking towards where the Baldwin pub will appear in 1935. To the left of the photographer a Co-op will be built around 1937.

Highfield Road looking north-east from the junction with Gresham Road, 19 September 1933. The man by the small vehicle on the left is selling English rabbits only.

Webb Lane, *c.* 1930. Even today, Webb Lane has a rural feel, especially at the holloway near the railway. Peter Bennett informs me that there is a coppice stool several centuries old at the Highfield Road end of the lane.

Paradise Lane, showing Paradise Farm, 9 February 1937. Gradually, the farm lost or sold all its land, and the farmhouse was finally demolished around 1960 and replaced by a low flat block.

Trittiford Park on a card posted in 1935. At a time when people did not go away so often for their holidays, local parks were very important to them. At Trittiford, apart from these lovely gardens, there was also a pavilion for refreshments, and boating could be done on the seven and a half acre pool in skiffs, with a motor boat available at weekends.

Three
Transport

The new tramlines to the Bull's Head, *c.* 1914. The last steam tram extension in the city had been to College Road in 1900, and steam trams ran until 31 December 1906, with electric trams taking over then, powered until 1912 by underground cable from Yardley. In the centre of the picture is the College Arms, built around 1913, and Greet Mill Hill Farm is just visible up the hill on Shaftmoor Lane.

The tram terminus at the Bull's Head on a card posted on 21 April 1924. From 31 May 1914 until 1 April 1928 this was as far as the trams went.

The tram terminus at the city boundary, c. 1928. Trams came as far as here from 2 April 1928 until 5 January 1937, using the central reservation.

The tramlines at the Robin Hood Inn, 13 May 1931. To the left are the grounds of Newey Goodman. This began in a small way in open country as George Goodman's Robin Hood Works, and eventually employed a thousand people making pins, grips, and fasteners, while retaining pleasant grounds with tennis courts. Most of the site is now covered by executive homes, the factory having closed around 1981.

A tram making its way up the hill from the river, c. 1935.

A transport scene near the Robin Hood Theatre, *c.* 1935. Buses were always a feature alongside trams on the Stratford Road route, whether they were horse buses, failed early motorbus experiments, or the eventual diesel winners. Hall Green never saw trolley buses, as the cost of diesel buses was comparable by the time the decision was made to abandon trams. Buses could also be more flexible: there were already seven routes branching off the Stratford Road by then. According to Roy Minton, there was nearly an accident on the last evening of tram service. He recalls being in a no. 29 bus opposite the end of Sarehole Road, going past a tram, when it suddenly reared up and jumped the rails, forcing the bus to swerve. Another tram had to come down the hill and drag it up to the crossover at the Robin Hood Parade, as one bogie was still off the rails.

Construction of the railway embankment, 1906. This is the only view I know of that shows the ford and footbridge at Robin Hood Lane at its former junction with Wake Green Road. A thick post stands at the site of the ford. The view below was taken by the leaning sign.

The new railway embankment on a card posted on 9 August 1906. This view shows the line of trees which marks the former lane, continued by part of Marion Way on the other side of the railway. The embankment had to be left for over a year to drain and consolidate before trains could run on it.

73

Hall Green Station, *c.* 1910. The line was opened for goods traffic in 1907, and for passengers in 1908.

Yardley Wood opened in 1908 as a 'platform'. This was the GWR's term at the time for a length of platform which could take a complete train. Shorter lengths, 'halts', were serviced by 'rail-motors'. A rail-motor was a passenger coach with a mini steam locomotive built in at one end, and carried about fifty people. Both rail-motors and ordinary trains ran on this line. There were complaints about the poor illumination afforded by the lamps seen here.

Yardley Wood Station, 1 January 1937. This bridge was a bottleneck, and a new bridge was constructed alongside in that year.

A commuter train on its way to Moor Street at Hall Green Station, 1950s. The engine is a 2-6-2 'Prairie' tank. The station's goods yard served the Velocette factory. Freight traffic ceased on 6 May 1968. I would like to thank Rick Green for this and the next photo, and for help with the information.

A signalman at Hall Green, 1950s. He is alerting Spring Road with the gong that the next train is on its way. The signal box had twenty-nine levers. It closed in August 1984.

Edwards' haulage business, 1930s. This was located behind the Paradise Lane farm cottages from around 1926 to 1962, and there is still a transport yard there now. The family was in the cottages before the business was started (see p. 100). Here are, left to right: Henry Richard Edwards Jnr, Henry Richard Edwards Snr, -?-, Frank Grainger, and William John Edwards.

The new roundabout at the Robin Hood junction, 19 September 1933. In the early 1930s, there was much talk about traffic congestion, speeding, and the best way to control junctions. One-way traffic was one solution, applied experimentally to new layouts called 'gyratories' or 'round-abouts', of which this was one of the first anywhere. The trams ran through the middle of the large island constructed here. By late 1934 shrubs had been planted to beautify it. Roy Minton recalls a tram stop and shelter on the island, plus these seats. Before the traffic lights there today were provided, it was suicidal to cross by the roundabout as a pedestrian: now the lights often serve to confuse drivers! The Robin Hood island, the largest in Birmingham, became part of Birmingham folklore. Comedians used to joke about having to fill up before daring to go round it. Hall Green acquired long stretches of pleasant, tree-lined dual carriageways. The aim behind these was two sets of one-way traffic. However, drivers began to use both carriageways as two-way roads, and the city had to take action in 1933 to get them used as intended!

A no. 29 bus on Highfield Road, July 1931. This route to Kingstanding started on 6 February 1928 and was discontinued on 28 February 1971, being replaced here by a short route to the College Arms, and elsewhere as the 90/92.

Highfield Road looking towards the river, 18 March 1937. The footbridge to the right of the road bridge was provided in 1926 after complaints, but was made on the 'wrong side' of the road for rail travellers from Yardley Wood. Some bricks from the early nineteenth century road bridge were used in the 1986 replacement. Trittiford House is on the left: see pp. 99-100.

Four

Hall Green at Work

Thomas Reeves Jnr (1893-1981) on the drive at Trittiford Farm with a milk cart, 1 May 1913. Note the different spelling of the name.

A tipcart and horse at Trittiford Farm, *c.* 1910.

A heavy horse with cart at Trittiford Farm, *c.* 1918.

Ploughing the headland, Trittiford Farm, *c.* 1918.

Thomas Reeves Jnr on the first tractor at Trittiford, a Fordson, May 1919.

Milk cooling equipment in the courtyard at Trittiford, 9 June 1922. Water was carried up the steps, poured into the tub, and allowed to run down through the system.

Trittiford Mill, Lot 12 in the Yardley Estate sale catalogue of 1913. It was described as an 'important holding' with a house, and mill and farm buildings as follows: annealing shop, engine room fitted with a twenty hp vertical steam engine, a rolling room, a six hp water wheel, gig house, three-stall cow-house, coach-house, loose box, three-stall stable, harness room with loft over, and three piggeries.

Sanford & Co. Ltd, Hall Green Nursery on a card posted on 8 January 1906. This was located south of Cole Bank Road on the west side of the Stratford Road. Sanfords were there until around 1918, and others followed until after the war, when Cambrai Drive was built.

Hall Green Parade, built in 1913, on a card posted in July 1914.

The Market Place on a card posted on 2 March 1911. These shops on the Stratford Road at the corner of Cateswell Road were there by 1910. A post office appeared around 1913. Gradually, the houses between here and the Parade were converted into shops, the first one being McEwan's in 1923.

B. Bloxham's shop, 9 Market Place, dated June 1920. This is now 1158, Stratford Road. Bloxhams were there from around 1918 to around 1923.

Shops opposite the former end of Cole Bank Road, 22 June 1955. The Tuck Shop is on the right. The Outer Circle buses had two sharp bends to negotiate from Cole Bank Road to School Road before the two were aligned in the early 1960s.

Edwards' garage at the corner of School Road and the Stratford Road, 2 April 1925. The garage took over the old Charity School premises (see p. 105).

John Gilbert, milkman for the Co-op depot on the Stratford Road, 1953. The depot had opened in 1938. John's horse Christie, here in its Mayday finery, won best in its class at the Birmingham Horse Show that year. I am grateful to him for this photo and information. John is now a leading member of the River Cole and Chinn Brook Conservation Group.

Hall Green Station staff, c. 1925. Third from the left in the front row as we look is Harry Tatton's brother Eric.

Alterations at Robin Hood corner, August 1923.

The Lord Mayor's visit to Electricars, Webb Lane, August 1943. The contrast between the status and power of Councillor W.S. Lewis and the workman behind him is a delight. The objects at the front are batteries.

The occasion was to celebrate the completion of a consignment of two-ton capacity electric trucks for the Russian armaments industry. The board wishes good luck and a speedy victory to our Russian comrades. George Smith, the last works superintendent at the site, kindly loaned his album of company photos to me for this book. His future wife Violet is on the front truck on the right as we look.

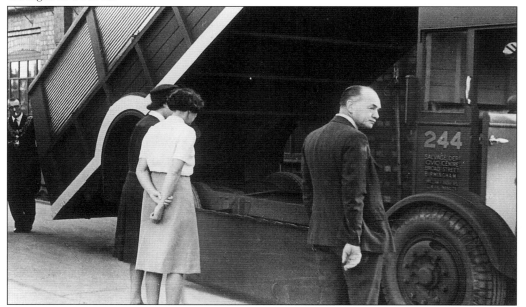

The Lord Mayor grabs a quick fag behind an electric refuse truck, manufactured here for the city.

Much of the Electricars album includes views of the factory before the war. These are the original buildings. Ken and Betty Hill of St Peter's Close gave me a copy of a conveyance in their deeds, showing that one Henry Crowder bought the land here late in 1910 in order to build a chocolate factory. A few years later his business had gone. By 1914 the factory was occupied by XL'ALL cycle saddles, followed by XL'ALL engines by 1919. By 1926 McKenzie Motors were making cars, and Thos. McKenzie was manufacturing baby carriages. The cars were not in the directories by 1930, but the prams were. By 1931 McKenzie was making invalids' furniture, MacBee were making signs, and the Rhode Motor Co. was making cars. The Woodwork Co. (Slough) Ltd was also here. By 1933 the motor manufacturer Star was listed as well, and the other company was Woodware. In 1938 Electricars is listed for the first time. They amalgamated with Morrisons of Leicester and Young Accumulators to form Associated Electric Vehicle Manufacturers. Later Crompton Parkinson became the owner. After the war the company was bought by BMC, who thought there might be a petrol shortage, and began making electric vehicles as a sensible investment. At the time, Electricars was the only British manufacturer of electrically powered heavy vehicles, supplying many corporations, docks, and companies. Electricars bought a company called Stacatruc and developed an electric forklift truck, clean for use in food distribution plants and elsewhere indoors. The factory was extended in the 1960s, and the business was then bought by an American company, Clark, who moved to Surrey a few years later. BMC had retained ownership of the site, and its last use was as a Rover development factory. It was replaced by housing in the 1980s. I am grateful to George Smith for much of the information here as well as the photographs of Electricars.

The Director's Office, 1938. It would seem a bit spartan to modern executives, I expect.

The Buying Office, 1938.

The Men's Canteen, 1938.

The Staff Dining Room, 1938.

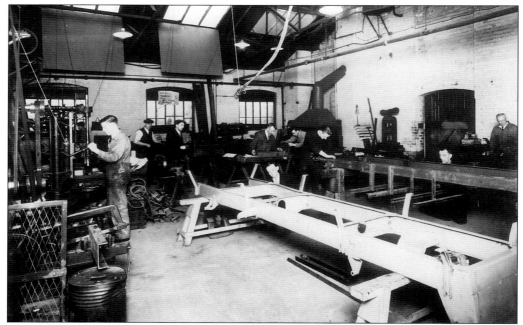

The Frame Shop, 1938. These frames are for 25-30 cwt utility vans.

Young workers at Luck's timber yard, Shaftmoor Lane, *c.* 1948. The company uses the old 1850 barn at Greet Mill Hill Farm as a mill. On 30 May 1959, a fire started, which destroyed two storage buildings and blistered paint on houses across the road. Fifty tons of timber were lost. Fortunately, firemen prevented the petrol station (built around 1947 where the pigsties had been) or the historic barn from being reached.

Lillian Wood as a young girl, exercising dogs at the Greyhound Stadium kennels, 1954. She worked there as one of the kennel maids. These girls groomed the dogs, clipped their nails, exercised them, paraded them, and fed them (tripe in the morning and meat an hour after racing: there was a mincing table and a meat boiler in the buildings). Until around 1970 there used to be four blocks of kennels, with a trainer and four kennel maids to each block. The kennels were outside the stadium, where the indoor cricket and bowls were in business until recently. There were up to forty dogs in these kennels at one time, some belonging to the Greyhound Racing Association, some to private owners. After races, dogs were allowed an hour to 'blow' in kennels inside the stadium.

Colleagues of Lillian Wood by the kennel blocks, 1954.

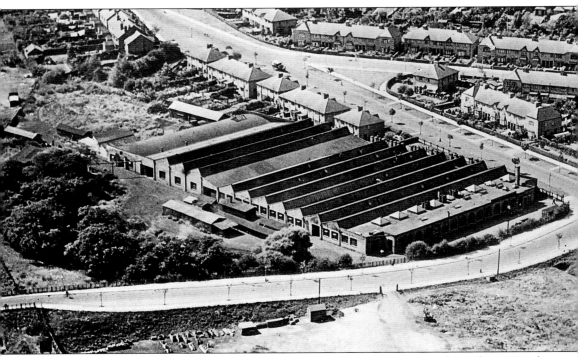

An aerial view of the Velocette factory, c. 1930. The company was formed in 1904 by a German, Johannes Gutgemann, who changed his name after 1914 to John Goodman. They moved from Aston to these larger premises in 1927 after one of their ohc bikes won the 1926 Junior (i.e. 350cc) TT by the amazing margin of ten minutes. Veloce was a family company of very skilled engineers and designers. The 350cc machine broke fifty world records in 1928, including averaging 100 mph for one hour. The 'K' series ohc bikes, designed by Percy Goodman and developed from the TT winner were in great demand, especially the KTT, which was the first racing bike made available over the counter by any British manufacturer. It soon became the first choice for privateers, i.e. riders not attached to works teams, and had legendary success in the racing world. Their MAC 350cc ohv pushrod single cylinder bike, designed by Eugene Goodman, was a great commercial success, selling for over thirty years. Eight TT's were won on Velocettes. After the war, there was a change of policy. In 1953 they pulled out of racing, and ceased making the KTT and the other ohc models. The company developed a new bike, which it was hoped would be a 'people's bike'. This was the LE, which was quieter but underpowered by comparison with the old Velocette favourites. The company invested heavily in the LE, but it proved popular only with the police, doing long hours on patrol: it became known as the 'Noddy bike'. Some achievements were still to come: world records in 1961, and the Production TT in 1967, the TT's Diamond Jubilee year. By the mid-1960s, there was heavy and as it turned out unjustified investment in another new type of machine. This was a large scooter, the Viceroy. Competition from Japan, new small cars, and poor labour relations also affected the company. Bertie Goodman was the last Managing Director, taking the company into voluntary liquidation in 1971. The Velocette name was bought by another company. Goodman Engineering lives on at Honeybourne. I am grateful to Simon Goodman for the photos and most of the technical information in these captions.

A 'K' series bike outside Veloce, early 1930s. Percy Goodman, the designer, is second from the right.

The works Mark VIII KTT, c. 1950. This bike, driven by Freddie Frith in 1949 and Bob Foster in 1950, won World Championships in those years, while Bertie Goodman was racing manager. It would cost you £20,000-£25,000 if you wanted to own a KTT now.

Bertie Goodman and colleagues at Montlhery, near Paris, March 1961. Eight riders, including Bertie Goodman, took the world record for twenty four hours on a 500cc machine on this occasion. They used a Venom Clubman, driving it at an average speed of over 100 mph, and taking five other world records on the way.

A Venom Thruxton, c. 1965. This was a high performance roadster designed by Bertie Goodman, and this example has the special dolphin type frontal fairing with perspex nose cone. Venom Thruxtons took first and second places in the 500cc class of the Production TT in 1967, with one doing the fastest lap of 91.01 mph.

Five
Portraits

Workers at Trittiford Farm, 1913. Left to right they are: Frank Holt, Thomas Reeves Jnr, Ted Reeves, and Tom Taylor.

Thomas Reeves Snr at Trittiford Farm, 17 August 1915.

Thomas Reeves Snr, Mary Reeves, and Ada Reeves, 28 July 1938.

The Clift family of Trittiford House Farm, *c.* 1893. The farmhouse stood by the garage near Yardley Wood Station. Back row: Fred Gillman, son of Mary, of Yew Tree Farm, Scribers Lane (1879-1936), Gertrude Hoskins, daughter of Joseph Bellamy Hoskins (1881-1961), Henry J. Bissaker Hoskins, known as Lal, son of Joseph Bellamy Hoskins, Joseph Bellamy Hoskins (1852-99), Thomas Clift, father of Thomas James Clift (1852-1913), Thomas James Clift (1874-1957), father of Norah Clift, who kindly provided this photograph and information, Ebenezer Thomas (Tom) Davies of Barton Lodge Farm (1875-1955). Middle row: Mary Gillman, daughter of Thomas Clift Snr (1855-1915), Rebecca Hoskins, daughter of Joseph Bellamy Hoskins, Rebecca Hoskins, wife of Joseph Bellamy Hoskins (1856-1921), Rebecca Clift, nee Bissaker, mother of Thomas Clift (1828-1902), Thomas Clift Snr, father of Thomas Clift (1831-1919), Louisa Maria Clift, nee Attwood, wife of Thomas Clift (1851-1904), Leah Rebekah Clift, daughter of Thomas Clift (1882-1951), Ann Davies, later Mrs Todd, sister of Ebenezer Thomas Davies. Smaller children in front of Thomas and Rebecca Clift: Daisy Hoskins, daughter of Joseph Bellamy Hoskins (1886-?), Victor Harold Clift, son of Thomas Clift (1887-1925), Sidney Clift, son of Thomas Clift, later Colonel Sir Sidney Clift, whence the Clifton Cinemas chain (1885-1951), Harold Ernest Clift, son of Thomas Clift (1891-1945), Madelina Norah Clift, daughter of Thomas Clift (1883-1953). The Clifts were at Trittiford House from around 1885 until the mid-1920s.

Thomas Clift Snr and Mary Gillman, c. 1905.

William John Edwards, Henry Richard Edwards Jnr, Emma Edwards (nee Birch), Kate Edwards, and Henry Richard Edwards Snr at the Ivy Cottage, 82 Paradise Lane (see also p. 76).

Roger Harris, said to be one of the best greyhound trainers in the city, *c.* 1960. He was a trainer at Hall Green from 1936, working for the Greyhound Racing Association for forty five years altogether. He died in 1973. His son Simon worked at Hall Green for eighteen years, for eight of these as racing manager. He is now at Wimbledon.

William Cuthbert Houghton, 1912. He was born in 1880. Dr Cuthbert appeared as a doctor in the 1909 directory, taking part of Kingswood (now 1094 Stratford Road), then moved to what became 1098. In 1912 a cousin, an architect, designed the large house at the former junction of Cole Bank Road and the Stratford Road (now occupied by a company). Dr Cuthbert gave it the same name of Crossways as his second house had had while he was there. The practice door was on the Stratford Road, and the house door on Cole Bank Road. As a young man, he was very slim, and one patient offered to pay him in advance, saying he looked as if he needed a square meal! During the influenza epidemic of 1919, Dr Houghton was allowed to take a partner, Dr Stubbs, who built 1025 Stratford Road, site of the present practice. Dr Cuthbert used to keep a donkey in fields nearby (see p. 17).

A.C., Helga, Guy, Ivan and Enid Houghton at Crossways, c. 1960. Both parents were doctors, and these three children followed them into the profession. A.C. Houghton was born on 28 October 1913. Christened Arnold Cecil, he was known as 'Micky' Houghton within the practice he joined in 1938, and as Timothy socially! He became chairman of the Birmingham Family Practitioner Committee and the Birmingham Local Medical Committee, and was awarded the OBE in 1976. Enid Houghton was born Enid Cyriax in London on 30 April 1913. Her grandfather, a German manufacturing chemist, was a friend of Wagner. Her mother was the daughter of a Swedish remedial gymnast, Jonas Henrik Kellgren, one of whose patients was Mark Twain. J.H. Kellgren's wife was Finnish, and was descended from the Russian von Jakovlev family: she had two uncles who were generals in the Russian army. Dr Cuthbert retired in 1956 to his holiday cottage in Silverdale, overlooking Morecambe Bay. He died in 1964. Dr Stubbs retired in 1958. Under the conditions of the Practice Agreement, both houses had to be sold to the on-going partnership. Dr Micky bought Crossways as a family home. The surgery suite was closed, and all consulting moved to 1025. A new purpose-built surgery was built in the garden of 1025 and opened in 1960. The original house became 1023, and was sold to become flats. Two pairs of semis were built on the rest of the garden fronting Greenbank Avenue. Dr Micky retired in 1984, and the family left Crossways in 1985 after the death of Enid's mother there at the age of 100. Many years before, Dr Micky had been interested in buying Hall Green Hall, but the asking price was too high for him … ah, what might have been! Dr Guy has been in the practice seen 1976, continuing the family tradition of service to Hall Green into a third generation, and is now senior partner. The 1960s premises have recently been extensively refurbished. I would like to thank Dr Guy for the photos and the family history.

Henry and Mair Goodall, who ran the dances at Highfield Hall, *c.* 1935. They were teachers of dancing as well. See also p. 115.

Francis Lawrence, *c.* 1935. He began as a milkman in Stirchley, then after the war worked for Liverpool Victoria insurance, becoming a well known face in the Lakey Lane and Pitmaston areas collecting contributions. He later became an inspector for the company.

Mr and Mrs J.J. Linthorn in retirement, 1962. They started their chemists business on the Stratford Road in 1926. There is now a chain of twelve shops with the name.

Don Young, c. 1950. He was one of the most respected figures in Hall Green's post war history. Born in 1910, he was a senior operational officer in the Fire Service in all Second World War air raids, a fire staff officer to the Control Commission in Germany from 1945-9, Chief Security Officer and Civil Defence Controller at BSA from 1949, and personnel manager there from 1960. He was a founder of the Industrial Police and Security Association, and a founder, president and chairman of the National Council of the International Professional Security Association. He was made an MBE in 1958, and his work for Hall Green Residents' Association is remembered with much admiration. He died in 1989.

Six

Schooldays

COLE BANK SCHOOL, HALL GREEN.

Cole Bank School, or the Charity School, *c.* 1905. A charity school from 1721 to 1881, it then became a public elementary school until around 1898, then a private high school until around 1910. After that it was a shop. From around 1918 it was occupied by Edwards' Garage. Atco Lawnmowers (1945-73) and Midas Exhausts used it before its demolition. The Horse Shoes pub can be seen next door.

A senior class of 1910 at Hall Green Board School, Stratford Road. The widow of John Drabble, third from the left in the second row as we look, donated the picture to the school. The school opened in 1893, and many photos were lent for its centenary: some are in this section. The school was extended from 1926-9, and in 1930 was split into Senior and Junior departments. From 1932 the Seniors went to Pitmaston, and the Juniors were split into Juniors and Infants.

The football team, Hall Green Board School, 1912-13.

The staff, Hall Green Council School, 1927. Harry Tatton recalls: back row: Mr Burgess, Miss Parsons, -?-, Mr Goodbody, -?-, Miss Pinfield, -?-. Front row: -?-, Miss Burford, Mr Peppiette (Head), Mr Hill, -?-.

Boys' gymnastics display at Hall Green Council School, c. 1928. Harry recalls: top row: -?-, -?-, -?-. Middle row: himself, Arnold Fowler, Norman Ward, Bob Fosbury, ? Sedgwick, George Middleton, Bob Thompson, Ralph Butcher. Front row: -?-, -?-, -?-, Fred Jelly, Alan Wiseman.

The infants' daisy chain dance, the February 1928 school concert. A detailed account of the concert, written by Joan Young, then 14, appeared in a local paper.

Land of the Dumps, or the Merry Beggars, a humorous sketch written by Mr Peppiette, the concert, 1928. Harry recalls: back row: -?-, -?-, Henry Lines, -?-, Vera Neale. Middle row: ? Sedgwick, Alan Croft, himself, -?-, George Middleton, Ralph Butcher, -?-, Madge Mountford, Brenda Ladbrooke. Front row: Graham Taylor, Grace Franklin, Edith Berry, Eva Morgan.

108

Hall Green Junior, girls, 1931.

Hall Green Junior, boys, *c.* 1930.

Hansel and Gretel, Hall Green School Parents' Day, 1937. Between them, Alan Johnson and Derek Hickson recall some of the children as follows: back row: -?-, -?-, Graham Gilbert, Geoffrey ?. Next row: -?-, -?-, -?-, Derek Hubner. Long row: Barry Wolstenhome, -?-, Jacqueline Horsley, Derek Smith, -?-, Roy Pountney, Alan Johnson, with Cynthia Lugsdin and Derek Hickson as the parents. Front row: Peter Thompson, Peter Webb, Margaret Sparks, Colin Nock.

Hall Green Junior Parents' day, 1939. Derek Hickson recalls: back row: Colin Nock, -?-, ? Jackson, Harry Smith, himself, Gerald Worthington, -?-, Roy Pountney, Peter Thompson, -?-. Second row: -?-, -?-, Derek Smith, -?-, -?-, -?-, Chris Busby, -?-, -?-. Third row: -?-, -?-, Margaret Chambers, -?-, -?-, -?-, -?-, -?-, -?-, -?-, Archie Bannocks. Fourth row: -?-, -?-, -?-, -?-, -?-, -?-, -?-, Audrey Rowe, John Edkins, -?-. Front row: -?-, Irene Paul, -?-, -?-, -?-, -?-, Margaret Stallard, -?-, Margaret Sparks, -?-.

A party at Rosslyn School, c. 1960. The boy fourth from the left is Nigel Mansell, who became one of Britain's greatest racing drivers.

St Boniface preparatory school, c. 1936. The school was at the corner of the Stratford Road and Wycome Road. John Barry Gilbert is in the back row, fourth from the right. Thanks to Graham Gilbert for this photo and the one below, and the information.

Party at St Boniface School, 1932. Josephine Betty Wiltshire is second from the left, and John Barry Gilbert second from the right in the back row.

Seven
Social Life

The Rialto cinema, *c.* 1928. Green Bank House, known for a while as 'Stuttering Hall' was demolished when this was built. The owner, Benjamin Beasley, had cured himself of a stammer, and proceeded to cure others at his house. It was originally a private school for young ladies some two hundred years ago. The Rialto opened on 3 October 1927, at the corner of Greenbank Avenue and the Stratford Road, with 960 seats. It closed on 30 May 1959, and was replaced by a supermarket.

The Robin Hood Theatre, *c.* 1935. This impressive 1,447 seat cinema was also a fully equipped theatre. It opened at the corner of the Stratford Road and Ingestre Road on 26 December 1927 with *Ben Hur*, and closed on 7 March 1970. It was also replaced by a supermarket.

Tennis at Highfield Hall, *c.* 1930. The first incarnation of Highfield Hall was as a pavilion for the Gresham and Highfield Hard Court Tennis Clubs. Until 1928 the land had been owned by Charles Lane.

A wedding reception at Highfield Hall, 1933. The Hall was originally one room, with today's dividing screens coming later. From around 1932 Henry and Mair Goodall ran a highly successful dancing business there. See also p. 103. Others in the family did the catering and the supervision of the customers. There was an annexe with Lloyd Loom tables and chairs for dancers to sit out and enjoy refreshments. It cost 1s 6d for four hours of live music from a band. No alcohol was sold on the premises, and those who wanted a drink had to get a pass-out ticket, and were refused re-admission if they were too merry when they returned. Dances opened with Bugle Call Rag. There were parties, lectures and meetings there, including those of the Residents' Association. During the war, Highfield Hall was requisitioned to store flour or dried milk. After 1945, Henry Goodall tried to recreate the business he had had before, but in 1955 he sold the site to the city. Requests were made at that time to turn the building into a community centre, but the council wanted to use the land for school buildings and playing fields, as they planned to widen the Stratford Road at the Junior School and knock the front part of it down. Since 1980 Highfield Hall has been used as a community centre and adult education centre, with a few years as a Citizens' Advice Bureau at the same time. The Residents' Association meet there once more.

Moor Green FC at New Street Station, 18 April 1933. They are returning from Belgium after defeating Eindhoven 3-1 to win the Verviers Cup, a forerunner of the European Cup. They won it again in 1937, both times as an amateur team playing against professional teams from Europe (at that time England refused to send professional teams). The club was founded in 1901, and played at various grounds in Moseley and Kings Heath, staying at Windermere Road for twenty-two years from 1908. George Fisher, an estate agent, became Secretary after a leg injury, and acquired fifty acres of land where Sherwood, Painswick and Bibury Roads are now (Oldhouse Farm). He sold forty-three acres for building, and kept the rest. He rented the 'Moorlands' to the club, and finally sold it to them in 1964. The new ground was opened in 1930. The club became professional in 1974 when strictly amateur football was abandoned as a principle by the FA. The club has been home to joint services by the Church of England, Methodist, Baptist and Congregational churches, and the Society of Friends also met there from time to time, all this before the war. More recently, a bridge club, quiz league, classical guitar club, and a folk club have met in the clubroom. Moseley Cricket Club played there until 1953, and other clubs until 1986, when floodlights were erected (the pitch had to be turned round to prevent the lights being a nuisance to residents) and a larger car park was provided. I am indebted to Peter Clynes for the photos of the club and all the information presented here.

Moor Green FC, 1935-36. This was the year they won the Birmingham AFA League Championship. Back row, directors and officials: A. Instone, A.G.A. Ayres, C.A. Perkin, F. Rawson, S. Johnson, H.C. Wilkins, W.B. Fletcher, E.J. Davies, S.B. Gane, W.S. Underhill, G.F. Fisher (inset, mentioned above). Middle row: A.G. Prosser, J.D. Edwards, D.H. Warwick, J.E. Whitehead, J.K. Hacking, A.J. Nasymth, L.G. Read, K.B. Burrow, E.G. Cutler, C.F. Blythe, V.E. Manley, J.H. Fisher. Front row: M. Curley, N.F. Love, C.J. Hirons, A.G. Rodway, A.W. Baverstock, G.W. Dance, E.A. Dare, T.H. Leek, A.P. Burgess, T.H. Stanley, W.T. Jones, L.G. Shepherd, A. Kirby (hon. trainer). E.A. Dare, known as Peter, was from the well-known family of builders. He became an RAF pilot and was killed in August 1941. Tommy Leek was the club's only (amateur) international, winning his first cap this season.

The stand at the new ground, opened 18 October 1930.

Hall Green YMCA Football Team, 1945-46, winners of the South Birmingham Youth and Old Boys' Shield. Dennis Wragg, the tall man in the back row, provided this photo. He recalls Alan Shimpton, Frankie Broome, Ernie Hunt and the Marston brothers in the team. They played where the Fox Hollies Leisure Centre pitches are now, between Fox Hollies and Shirley Roads.

The Civil Service Bowling Club, 1942. Harry Tatton recalls: back row: Charlie Bratton, Jim Wright, Stan Mason, himself, -?-, -?-, Joe Elmes, Bill Gilbert, Horace ?, Bill Hughes, Dave Pratt, -?-, Bill Thomas, Horace Poulton, Alan Denning. Middle row: Wal Hughes, George Bateman, Sandy Powell, Revd Gunson, Ernie Howarth, J.W. Smith, C. Camps, -?-, Charlie Payne, -?-, Bill Colvin. Front row: B. Thomas's son, S. Powell's son, Mrs G. Mason, -?-, Mrs Thomas, Mrs Howarth, -?-, Mrs W. Hughes, Mrs Colvin, -?-, Mrs Minnie Powell.

Betty Williams, Mary Gaze, Eve Rodway, and Meg Chambers, Division Four winners, LTA League, at Sparkhill Tennis Club, c. 1946. Now renamed Hall Green Tennis Club, it moved from Sparkhill to Petersfield Road in 1928.

The Men's Fellowship at Hall Green Church, late 1940s.

A mothers' and children's group at the church, late 1940s.

Hall Green Church Fellowship ramble, Easter Monday 1939. The Revd Percy Chatterton is seated behind the man whose legs come furthest forward at the front.

An evening service at Pitmaston School, late 1940s.

The Arcadians, a play performed by the Church Fellowship, late 1940s.

A coach-built motor caravan being constructed on a 1933 taxi chassis at Brooklands Road, 1952. The owner, Rick Green, still runs this vehicle now. After a distinguished career in local government, Mr Green is now known for his railway books. He has kindly provided a couple of railway photos for this book.

The first church on the Stratford Road Baptist Church site, opened 17 April 1926. After two years at the Friends Meeting House, a congregation was formed in 1914. The land was acquired in 1922. Behind is Ferndale Road.

The laying of the foundation stone for the new church, 2 March 1935. The Lord Mayor, Alderman S.J. Grey (a deacon of Acocks Green Baptist church), presided. The doors were opened on 25 January 1936, by Mrs W.A. Cadbury, JP. The interior was altered in 1975.

Baptist church, Men's Circle outing to Malvern, 1946. Back row: George Hall, -?-, George Mannering, Mr Roberts, Raymond Pearson, Herbert Smith, Jack Lewis, Howard Dudley, Arthur Dudley, John Daulby, -?-, Norman Dodman, Ted Pipe, David Thirsk, Revd Eric Knight, -?-, Walter Stevens, Archie Hitchman, Mr Vaughan. Front row: Frank Yarrington, Ernest Lugsdin, Len Hallam, Stan Twiby, Tom Beckett, -?-, Ted Woolley, Les Parker, Bert Gibson, Harry Saunders, W.C. Lacey, Dick Edson, Billie Inman. The Baptist church has always played a strong role in the community, and its halls are home to a great variety of activities as well. It played an important part in the establishment of the Hall Green Council of Churches, which created the programme to bring Belfast children from both religious communities to Hall Green each summer.

A family scene in the garden at the Birches, *c*. 1912. The Smith family lived there at the time. Thomas Smith was a horse dealer and breeder.

The lily pond, the Birches, *c*. 1912.

Tree seat, the Birches, *c.* 1912.

An outing from the Birches, *c.* 1912.

The Greyhound Stadium, *c.* 1950. It opened on 24 August 1927, with 20,000 people attending. The site had been bought at the end of 1926 from William Welch, who had developed it as the Olympia Sports Ground. Over 2,400 local residents signed a petition objecting to the proposed stadium. In 1928 they found a new cause for objection when motorcycle speedway racing, a sport new to Britain, started on a circuit inside the greyhound track. A debate ensued in the local papers about whether the combined rates paid by objectors came to more than the combined rates paid by the stadium and those who enjoyed the racing! Speedway finished when the Second World War started. Eventually a soccer pitch was made in the centre area. The totalisator board seen here appeared after the war, and was taken down around 1970. A restaurant stand was built in 1970, and the main stand was replaced around 1975. Substantial investment has continued to take place, with a snooker club (1986), motel, restaurant and conference and other rooms now on site. By 1970 the kennels outside the track (see p. 93) had been replaced by private kennels, and warehouses subsequently appeared in their place, occupied by various businesses, including a cash and carry, indoor cricket, indoor bowls, and a wood yard, the latter the only one currently in operation.

The visit of the Prince of Wales, Stratford Road, June 1923. Dr Mitchell has only recently moved into the house seen here. In the mid-1930s a row of businesses, including the Co-op's shops and milk distribution depot, will be built to the right of the house.

Coronation festivities at Chilcote Close, 1953. The Harvey family, who lent this photo, moved there in 1952 from prefabs in Brookwood Avenue.